FOR THE LOVE

from A to Z

OF BASKETBALL

written by **Frederick C. Klein** art and design by **Mark W. Anderson**

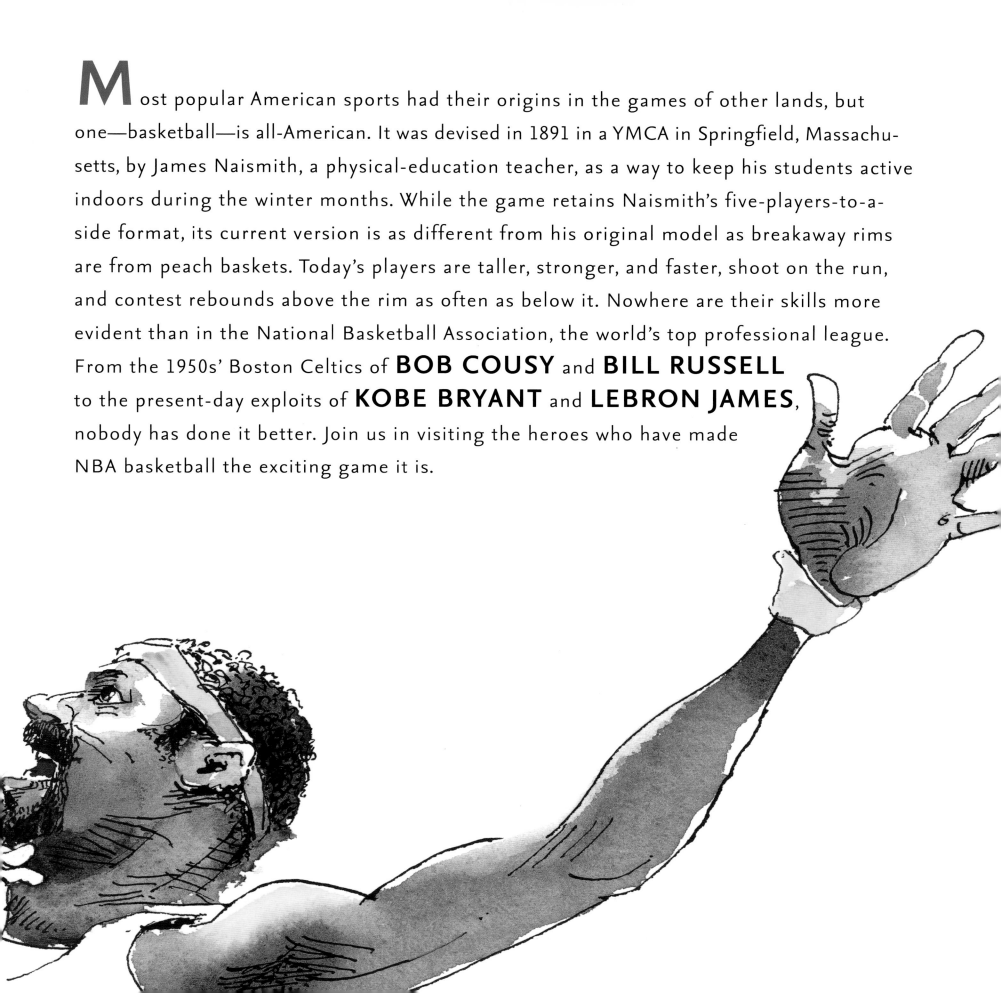

Most popular American sports had their origins in the games of other lands, but one—basketball—is all-American. It was devised in 1891 in a YMCA in Springfield, Massachusetts, by James Naismith, a physical-education teacher, as a way to keep his students active indoors during the winter months. While the game retains Naismith's five-players-to-a-side format, its current version is as different from his original model as breakaway rims are from peach baskets. Today's players are taller, stronger, and faster, shoot on the run, and contest rebounds above the rim as often as below it. Nowhere are their skills more evident than in the National Basketball Association, the world's top professional league. From the 1950s' Boston Celtics of **BOB COUSY** and **BILL RUSSELL** to the present-day exploits of **KOBE BRYANT** and **LEBRON JAMES**, nobody has done it better. Join us in visiting the heroes who have made NBA basketball the exciting game it is.

A is for **A-J,**
Mister Abdul-Jabbar.
The teams that he led
Would always go far.

Kareem Abdul-Jabbar was the most prolific scorer in basketball history and one of the game's most successful players. As a teen in his native New York, the lanky center led Power Memorial Academy to Catholic League titles in each of his three high school varsity years. Then he went west to UCLA, where three of his teams won NCAA championships (1967–1969). As a pro he acquired a ring with the 1971 Milwaukee Bucks, his initial club, and five more with the Los Angeles Lakers, to which he was traded in 1975. Thanks largely to his unstoppable "sky hook," he ended his career in 1989 as the National Basketball Association's leading scorer with 38,387 points. He was a six-time NBA Most Valuable Player and a 19-time All-Star.

B is for

Bird,

Whose game could take wing.
He'd fake an opponent,
Then make the twines sing.

Larry Bird was raised in the small Indiana towns of West Baden and French Lick and was so unused to urban ways that he found big-school Indiana University frightening and dropped out after less than a month. Eventually, he enrolled in and starred at smaller Indiana State University, then took his game to new heights in his 13 seasons with the NBA's Boston Celtics. A deadeye shooter with unequalled court awareness, he helped the Celtics to titles in 1981, 1984, and 1986, and was a three-time NBA MVP. He retired in 1992 after playing with the U.S. Olympic "Dream Team," the greatest basketball unit ever assembled.

C is for **Cousy**,

**Of old Celtic glory.
Six championship rings
Were part of his story.**

Bob Cousy learned basketball on the New York playgrounds during the 1940s, honing moves that would transform the game at the College of Holy Cross and with the Celtics in his 1951–1963 tenure in Boston. Basketball in his day was mostly a set-piece affair, dominated by big men and structured plays. He introduced behind-the-back dribbling and no-look passes that produced baskets as well as a good show. The Celtics won six NBA titles under the slim point guard's leadership (1957, 1959, 1960, 1961, 1962, and 1963), establishing the league's first dynasty.

D is for

Drexler and
Duncan—

The "Texas Connection."
Each gave his lineup
A perfection injection.

Houston native **Clyde "the Glide" Drexler** made his first national basketball splash as a member of the University of Houston's celebrated "Phi Slamma Jamma" team, which made NCAA Final Four appearances in 1982 and 1983. The acrobatic, 6'7" guard then gained All-NBA status with the Portland Trail Blazers. He later returned to Houston and helped the Rockets win the 1995 title. Tim Duncan, from the Virgin Islands, was the collegiate Player of the Year at Wake Forest University before coming to the San Antonio Spurs in 1997. Big, agile, durable, and unflappable in big-game situations, he led the Spurs to their first NBA crown in 1999, and repeated the performance in 2003, 2005, and 2007.

E is for

Erving,

The great "Dr. J."
His aerial feats
Amaze to this day.

The American Basketball Association, started in 1967, offered a faster, freer-flowing game than that of the established NBA, and **Julius Erving** was its biggest star. Popping eyes nightly with his spectacular and innovative dunks and boasting a solid fundamental game as well, "the Doctor" led ABA teams to three league titles. He continued his brilliance with the Philadelphia 76ers after the leagues merged in 1976, culminating in the Sixers' 1983 championship-round sweep of the Lakers. His 30,026 pro-career points are fifth on the all-time list.

F is for Frazier_

This "Clyde" was bonny.
His Knicks in the '70s
Raked in the money.

Walt Frazier, nicknamed "Clyde" after the gangster portrayed in the movie Bonny and Clyde, was the prototypical professional point guard, equally adept at scoring and setting up teammates to score. His flamboyant fashion sense further endeared him to the New York public. With Frazier at the controls the New York Knickerbockers enjoyed their greatest success, winning NBA championships in 1970 and 1973. That team, which also included Willis Reed, Bill Bradley, Earl Monroe, and Dave DeBusschere, often is ranked among the league's greatest fives.

G is for

Gervin –

"The Iceman" was cool.
Over 14 pro seasons
He took foes to school.

At 6'7" **George Gervin** was tall for a guard when he showed up to play with the ABA's Virgina Squires in 1973. He was also skinny, but nobody could stop him that year or in the next 13 of his pro career, 11 of them with the Spurs. Not only could he shoot over opponents, he went around and under them as well, and his scooping "finger roll" layup became his signature shot. He was a 12-time ABA or NBA All-Star, and his 26,595 career points puts him 13th all time.

H is for Havlicek,

Always on the run.
He showed that a "sixth man"
Could be Number 1.

John Havlicek was a star at Ohio State University, but when he arrived in the pros with the Celtics in 1962 he was judged to be a "tweener," too short (at 6'5") to play the forward position he manned in college and not quick enough for the backcourt. No problem, though; he invented his own position of "sixth man"—first off the bench—and made it pay with his hustle, defensive skills, and keen shooting eye. He'd go on to play 16 seasons in Boston and collect eight championship rings. In 1997 he was selected as one of the NBA's 50 greatest players ever.

I is for **Iverson**,

Slim as a reed,
But he was propelled by
A will to succeed.

Allen Iverson was another player who didn't fit the mold for NBA stardom; at barely 6'0" and a listed 165 pounds, he seemed too small and frail to survive the league's rigors. That was made worse by the fact that he preferred to mix it up with the big men around the hoop rather than remain outside the fray. But every time he was knocked down he got back up, and in a long pro career, mostly with the 76ers (1996–2006), he made repeated All-Star Game appearances, won four scoring titles, and was the 2001 MVP.

J is for

Jordan

Bottom line: The Best.
His skills, grit, and spirit
Exceeded the rest.

The NBA abounds in great athletes, but, by acclamation, the best of them has been Michael Jordan. Drafted No. 3 in 1984 by the Chicago Bulls out the University of North Carolina, the 6'6" guard first was celebrated for his physical skills, but as he aged he developed the rest of his game until he had no peer in any department. Further, his thirst for victory and work ethic were unmatched, and he constantly prodded his teammates to follow his example. Even with Jordan it took the Bulls seven seasons to win their first NBA crown, in 1991, but from there they won it five more times in seven years (in 1992, 1993, 1996, 1997, and 1998), with Jordan the MVP in each of those final series. He made sports-business history as well with his "Air Jordan" shoe line for Nike and in 2010 headed a group that bought the Charlotte Bobcats, becoming the first ex-player to have a controlling interest in an NBA team.

K is for

Kobe,

"Jelly Bean's" boy.
He's made the title trophy
His personal toy.

Kobe Bryant is the son of Joe "Jelly Bean" Bryant, a former NBA player. Kobe spent part of his youth in Italy and Spain, where his father played professionally. He was a first-round draft pick out of a suburban Philadelphia high school in 1996 at age 18 and along with Shaquille O'Neal led the Los Angeles Lakers to titles in 2000, 2001, and 2002. More titles have followed in L.A. under Bryant's leadership, in 2009 and 2010. He's a four-time NBA scoring champ, and his 25,790 career regular-season points at the end of the 2010 season topped the Lakers' all-time list.

L is for

LeBron,

The "All-Everything" kid.
No youngster before him
Did the things that he did.

LeBron James is another player who went straight from high school to the pros at age 18. He did it with more hoopla than any previous youngster and with a $90 million shoe contract in hand. The 6'8", 250-pounder was amazingly mature for his age, and his fast, powerful game made him an instant sensation. He averaged almost 21 points per game in his rookie year with the Cleveland Cavaliers and improved steadily thereafter to join Kobe Bryant as the best of the current-day players. His decision to join the Miami Heat as a free agent during the 2010 off-season was so eagerly awaited that an hour-long, national-television special was staged for the announcement.

M is for "Magic,"

Also "Mailman" Malone.
They're up with the best
The game's ever known.

Earvin "Magic" Johnson and **Karl "Mailman" Malone** were two of the best players of their overlapping eras. Johnson was a 6'9" guard who could do everything the best big and "small" players could do. He teamed with Kareem Abdul-Jabbar to bring championships to the Lakers in 1980, 1982, 1985, 1987, and 1988, and was a 12-time All-Star. His sunny personality endeared him to fans everywhere. The big, rugged Malone was the model power forward in his 18 seasons (1986–2003) with the Utah Jazz. His 36,928 regular season points put him second behind Abdul-Jabbar on the career scoring list.

N is for

Nash,

The Canadian flash.
This ballhandling wizard
Doesn't lack for panache.

Canada is known for producing hockey players, not ballers, but Steve Nash, who grew up in Victoria, British Columbia, broke the mold. Drafted by the Phoenix Suns out of Santa Clara University in 1996, the swift point guard made little initial impact and in 1998 was traded to the Dallas Mavericks. He blossomed there for six seasons, then returned to Phoenix as a free agent and attained full-blown stardom, winning league MVP awards in 2005 and 2006. His popularity in his native country is such that he was selected to light the Olympic cauldron at the start of the 2010 Winter Games in Vancouver.

O is for O'Neal,

A mountain in shorts.
When he calls himself "Superman,"
Nobody snorts.

Shaquille O'Neal is a big man who stands out even in a sport well stocked with them, a 7'1", 300-plus-pounder whose strength and girth impresses even fellow players. An intimidating defender and possessing a variety of close-in offensive moves, he made an instant title contender of his first NBA team—the Orlando Magic—and went on to win championships with the Lakers and Heat. Off the court, he has spoofed himself in a variety of movie roles. He's said he wants to get into law enforcement once his playing days are done.

P is for

"Pistol;"

That's Pete Maravich.

His artistry earned him

A Hall of Fame niche.

Pete Maravich's father, Press, was a coach, and he handed his son a basketball while the boy was a toddler. "Pistol" Pete went on to do things with it that nobody had, before or since. Maravich's "showtime" style included dipsy-do ballhandling, a range of blind passes, and shots from angles other players wouldn't attempt. He broke all the national collegiate scoring records playing for his dad at Louisiana State University and continued to dazzle over 10 NBA seasons (1971–1980) before injuries cut short his career. He died suddenly at age 40 of a heart attack while playing in a pick-up basketball game.

Q is for the Question:

Which dynasty would rule?
There's really no answer,
So jump in the pool.

The NBA has had a number of teams that dominated the game for extended periods. The longest-running dynasty was the **Bob Cousy–Bill Russell** Celtics, which won 11 league titles in 13 years (1957–1969). The Lakers, led by **Kareem Abdul-Jabbar** and **Magic Johnson**, dominated the 1980s, winning in 1980, 1982, 1985, 1987, and 1988. **Michael Jordan**'s Bulls won six times in eight years in the 1990s (1991–1993 and 1996–1998). The Lakers have won five times in the new century (2000–2002 and 2009–2010), and **Tim Duncan**'s San Antonio Spurs took four championships in a scattered reign (1999, 2003, 2005, and 2007). Which of those teams were best? We'll never know but we can always argue about it. That's one of the great things about sports.

R is for

Robertson and
Russell—

Bright stars, all agree.
One was the "Big O,"
The other "Big D."

Oscar "Big O" Robertson was one of the top players of the 1960s and early 1970s, a big, sturdy guard who did everything well. First with the Cincinnati Royals and then the Milwaukee Bucks, he posted 30-plus scoring averages in each of six seasons and was among the annual league leaders in assists and rebounding. During his 1962 rookie year he averaged a triple double, a rare feat for even a single game. **Bill Russell**, a career Celtic (1957–1969), owns 11 championship rings, the most of any player. A defensive specialist known for his shot-blocking and rebounding, the sinewy center was the glue for Boston's long-running supremacy. His duels with Wilt Chamberlain make up a vivid chapter in league lore.

S is for Stockton;

His weapon: the pass.
For setting up baskets
He was in his own class.

At 6'1" and 170 pounds, **John Stockton** was judged by many to be too small to succeed in the NBA, and maybe too slow as well, but his hard-nosed style and appreciation of the game's geometry turned him into one of its all-time best point guards. In 19 seasons with the Jazz (1985–2003) he established league records for most assists (15,806) and steals (3,265) while consistently scoring in double figures. He and Karl Malone formed one of the game's best-ever outside-inside combinations.

T is for Thomas,

The "Bad Boy"-in-chief;
On offense a marksman,
On defense a thief.

Basketball never has been the non-contact sport defined in the rulebook, but no team has gone further playing what's known as "physical" defense than the 1980s Detroit Pistons. Their ringleader was **Isiah Thomas**, a clever, versatile point guard drafted in 1981 after winning an NCAA title at Indiana University. Supported by such muscular henchman as Bill Laimbeer, Rick Mahorn, and Dennis Rodman, the Thomas-led "Bad Boys" won their city's first NBA crown in 1989 and repeated the next year. Thomas ended a 13-year pro career among the league leaders in assists and steals while averaging 19 points per game.

U is for
Unseld,
Neither fast nor real tall,
But more often than not
He'd come up with the ball.

Even in the 1970s, 6'7" wasn't tall for an NBA front courter, but wide-beamed **Wes Unseld** knew what to do with his frame, and used it to grab rebounds and set picks for the Baltimore and Washington Bullets teams that were consistent title contenders during his tenure (1969–1981). Unseld's Bullets made four final-series appearances in that period and won the 1978 championship, with him as the finals' MVP. He later was a head coach and executive with the team.

V is for the Van Arsdales–

The twins, Dick and Tom.
To tell them apart
You'd have to ask Mom.

Dick and **Tom Van Arsdale** are identical twins who had nearly identical basketball careers. They shared Indiana All-State and "Mr. Basketball" honors at Indianapolis Manual High School, then went on to star at Indiana University. Each was a second-round pick in the 1965 NBA draft, had a 12-year pro career (1966–1977), and was a three-time All-Star. They had similar career points-per-game averages in the pros—Dick's at 16.4, and Tom's at 15.3. They played on different clubs for most of their time in the league, but teamed up for their last season with the Phoenix Suns.

W is for Wilt,

Who called his own tune.
He was, when he chose,
A scoring typhoon.

Few players have dominated their eras the way **Wilt "The Stilt" Chamberlain** dominated his. Bigger, stronger, and more athletic than just about anyone he faced, the 7'1" center won scoring titles his first seven years in the NBA (1960–1966) and became the only player to average more than 50 points in a season (50.4 in 1962) and score 100 points in a game. When his point producing paled he turned his hand to rebounding and won 11 titles before retiring in 1973. Once—just to show he could— he led the league in assists. Alas for him, most of his teams futilely chased the Celtics in the standings, but two of them did win championships—the 1967 Sixers and the 1972 Lakers.

X is a mark

Coaches make on a slate.
The NBA's had its share
Of skippers who rate.

Phil Jackson has won the most titles of any NBA coach—six with the Bulls and five (so far) with the Lakers. **Walter "Red" Auerbach** won nine with the Celtics before turning over the team's reins to **Bill Russell**, who won two more. **Pat Riley** guided both Lakers and Heat teams to championships. **Gregg Popovich** was in charge for each of the four Spurs' crowns. Lots of other good coaches have worked in the league. With its 82-game regular schedule and two months of playoffs, it's a yearly marathon for them as well as for their players.

Y is for **Yao**,

**So far from the floor
That he has to stoop
To get through a door.**

There have been players taller than 7'6" **Yao Ming**, but no one his height has matched his skills and stamina. The native of Shanghai, China, was the first player chosen in the 2002 NBA Draft, by the Houston Rockets, and was picked to play in the All-Star Game in each of his first seven NBA seasons. He missed 2009–2010 with a foot injury but was expected to be back the next season. His play has helped increase global awareness of the U.S. professional game.

Z is for "Zeke,"

Whose form was so fine
The NBA made it
Its signature line.

Jerry West was so rustic when he joined the Lakers in 1960 that his teammates nicknamed him "Zeke from Cabin Creek," after the stream that ran through his tiny home town of Chelyan, West Virginia. The guard's game was thoroughly big time, though, and he quickly became the team's floor leader and an All-Star Game fixture in his 14 seasons in Los Angeles. Further, the silhouette of him bringing the ball up court was adopted as the NBA's logo and graces each player's uniform and league-endorsed products. After his playing days West had a successful front-office career with the Lakers and Memphis Grizzlies.

This book is available in quantity at special discounts for your group or organization. For further information, contact:

Triumph Books
542 South Dearborn Street
Suite 750
Chicago, Illinois 60605
312. 939. 3330
Fax 312. 663. 3557
www.triumphbooks.com

Printed in China
ISBN 978–1–60078–541–2